The Ascension of Sandy's Drive-In

The Ascension of Sandy's Drive-In

Poems by

Rodney Torreson

Cover design by Shay Culligan
Author photo by Steve Fortugaleza

ISBN: 978-1-63980-381-1

Kelsay Books
502 South 1040 East, A-119
American Fork, Utah 84003
Kelsaybooks.com

Acknowledgments

Thank you to the following publications, where versions of these poems previously appeared:

The American Journal of Poetry: "Jesse James in the Barber Chair on the Second Floor of a Vacant House"
Amethyst Review: "As If God Will Dress Me Down to Dust"
Artful Dodge: "From a Bench on Main Street in Ulysses Grant's Hometown, Galena"
The Aurorean: "How Bizarre That Snow Must Melt"
The Briar Cliff Review: "Iowa Snowstorm," "Lonely for the Old Gods (or for His Herd)," "Something Is Going on Far Back of the Ancient Lawn"
Canary: "Leaping Doe and Fawns Flash Before Us"
Cape Rock: "Down in the Lowlands below Motel 8," "Though They Didn't Know It, the Teenage Girls Who Stole My 80-Year-Old Mother's Walker"
Common Ground Review: "Two Sisters," "Tail Gator"
Connecticut River Review: "The Candling"
Cottonwood: "The Fires Actually Fought That Fall by the Volunteer Fireman"
The Courtship of Winds: "At St. Luke's Nursing Home"
Hamilton Stone Review: "The Man Who Delivered Flowers Along Leonard Street"
Ibbetson Street Magazine: "Goose Pond at Dusk"
Kansas Quarterly: "Banister"
The Listening Eye: "Old Barn"
Main Street Rag: "Father and I Out Driving, Not Knowing It Is the Last Time"
Mankato Poetry Review: "The Old Man Under the Sidewalk"
Margie: "Electric Fence"
The Mid-America Poetry Review: "Mother Helps Him Up to Play Pool at Senior Citizens"
Miramar: "It Would Be Fitting for a Small Town"

Natural Bridge: "Beneath Our Hickory the Blind Stranger Raps His Cane Against the Porch Screen"
Naugatuck River Review: "In a Fever the River Rose Over the Truss Bridge West of Emmetsburg"
Nebraska Territory: "The Ascension of Sandy's Drive-In," "While Father in the Hospital Re-Imagines His Hand"
Negative Capability: "Locked Room"
North Dakota Quarterly: "Along the Crumbling Sidewalk," "Real Poems: A Rush from Each One I Flag"
Northeast: "Backboard and Hoop," "When Father Castrated Hogs," "Wooden Ducks"
Painted Bride Quarterly: "Power Lines"
Paterson Literary Review: "For Brother Bill, Collector of Old Radios"
Plainsongs: "I Never Climbed a Tree"
Poet Lore: "Enough Cattle for Us to Be Alone," "September Night, 1969"
Porcupine: "Cary Grant Dies in Davenport, Iowa"
The Seattle Review: "As If a House Is Not Enough to Clean, Mother Swept the Mulberry Tree"
Seems: "Bone-to-Bone This Bouncing"
Slant: "Plane Ride with My Uncle"
Spoon River Quarterly: "Matthew Schmiel"
Streetlight Magazine: "Learning the Names of Flowers," "On a Blustery November Morning in Front of His Parents' Hardware Store"
Talking River Review: "Old License Plates," "Showdown on Carroll Street"
Tar River Poetry: "Impressions of a Roan-Colored Steer," "Dusk Draws More Dark the Closer They Approach on the Sidewalk"
Thema: "Improbable World"
Third Coast: "For Photos, Father Stretched His Right Hand Behind His Back," "Playing Back a Tree"

Third Wednesday: "Age 12, Beneath a Harvest of Stars and Driven by Murder," "The Plump White Rat that Paul and Margie Left Behind for Back Rent"
Tipton Poetry Review: "Karla Could Ply a Smile from a Storm Cloud, Get Sunlight to Flap Its Wings"
Town Creek Poetry: "I'd Heard About the River of Time," "On Summer Afternoons, Even as the Shadows Cast Their Nets"
Two Cities Review: "In the Wake of the Storm, When Snow Had Reached the Rooftops"
Whitefish Review: "The Lutheran Church in Graettinger, Iowa, Is Burning to the Ground"

*

"Backboard and Hoop" first appeared in *Full Court: A Literary Anthology of Basketball,* published by Breakaway Books and edited by Dennis Trudell.

"In the Parking Lot after Leaving the Mall," "Leaving Neighbors," "Storm" and "The Suitcase" first appeared in my chapbook *The Secrets of Fieldwork.*

"The Brooder House Rabbits" first appeared in *Undocumented, Great Lakes Poets Laureate on Social Justice,* edited by Ron Riekki and Andrea Scarpino.

*

My grateful acknowledgment to Russell Thorburn for ordering the poems in *The Ascension of Sandy's Drive-In* and for critiquing many of them as well. Thank you also to Matthew Brennan, David Allan Evans, Robert Haight, Alyssa Jewell, Miriam Pederson, and Barbara Saunier for their feedback on the individual poems.

Contents

I.

II.

III.

I.

Real Poems: A Rush from Each One I Flag on the Mailbox

My share of earth is not
limited to waiting. One day I'm
bumped up by acceptance
in lean prose—no superlatives, only
that they'll appear in POETRY NOW.
Not rankled by happiness
that can't last, I tip the rain barrel
back of the garage—
though branches are still beaded,
the sun lifting up the cracks
in the sidewalk before our house,
filling them in, as I stride
down the block, the old street breaking
through to where trees talk a tangent
in new leaves, as if I'd finally
found the password. I walk the curve
of the earth, my tennis shoes
bouncing, my swinging arms
a kind of signature as I take in
a higher traffic—wheels of sunlight
running me down if I stop
to rubberneck what I'd done,
so I keep moving, my ear soon
running to every clearing, as if I've
proof I'm part of thought culture,
planting more poems, each fence,
tired of holding back, climbs
the light like a lattice, or maybe
a kite, its light frame flying
on a string of wind.

Jesse James in the Barber Chair
on the Second Floor of a Vacant House

In the outskirts by the river
one Saturday my
fifth-grade pals and I
pushed in the door
to see the chair
that drew him in
a hundred years before,
leaving mere shadows
to be shot up in Northfield.

We were sure
that Jesse's atoms stayed
with that chair,
as we ran our hands
over the quantum silence
along its contours
and thought about days
when the sky was tree-ragged
and even Jesse
smoothed his life
through a haircut and shave.

Rust-flecked but steely,
this Jesse was enough.
Though his leather skin
chafed to dust,
we marveled at his
blank stare, the headrest,
and how boldly he'd bolted himself
to the floor, daring anyone
who stood behind him
on the twist
of hurling stairs.

Soon, we took turns climbing
onto Jesse's body,
pumping ourselves up—

that we were gunfighters too,
enjoying braggadocio
in standing
upon the hard cushion,
raising both hands,
to straighten the picture,
but almost as quickly we'd hop
off, for it looked a lot like
we were going to get shot
or we'd given ourselves up.

Cary Grant Dies in Davenport, Iowa

So far from Grace,
whose honey lips
should unlock another life,

he, drawn to Davenport
as if by the whir
of great harvesters.

Even on his last day
he throbs the Adler Theatre,
where women still feel
the raised nap of his gaze.
A few miles away
hogs snuffle a Mediterranean air;
cattle close their eyes
and dream of beaches.

Once, his skulking frame
tamed even shadows
as he vaulted along the roof
of that hotel on the Riviera,
owning every room,
charming windows
for years held enchanted by the sea—
enchanting us, too,
into perfect obedience
to the screen.

In his last hours,
how could he
check in at the Black Hawk
with its name's shameless
hacking at the rates,
at a hotel that launders
and folds the middle class?

Cary Grant dies in Davenport, Iowa,
old and overweight,
in a place far from the skin,
his dying there strange as that crop duster
buzzing out of nowhere:
no tips in the bed sheets
nor language of his lover's lipstick
in the mirror.

Somewhere an old woman
who waited too long
searches through the old films—
none led there.

I Never Climbed a Tree

except for one with its high limbs low
and then would climb down
the combination branches, my mouth
and hands purple with mulberries, never clambering
for climbing's sake, but admired taut
arms and legs required for taking command,
ascending the sloping boughs
with poise and balance to keep going
shin to shin on a tree's trapeze.
When a young poet stalled, I'd tell them
they might write about climbing a tree.
Maybe they did. But the yes kids
would get only a little higher than the ones
whose smiles would chafe at the notion,
until finally it happened, after I retired.
I sat across a restaurant booth from a teenage
girl with flashing blue eyes and ribbons
of laughter, one wrist feasting on bracelets
and under the table long legs that looked like
they could hold a table up, and calves
with bundled muscles, which made it look
like she could really go—a green but leafy
young poet—who'd already made it
into *Rattle* and the *Louisville Review*.
In no time she was up and scaling,
she and the wind both angling, matching
the hurtling of the knobby branches,
scrambling up every which way and me admiring
a brilliant girl who had branched
into other fields too. I didn't know,
but it was the last time she'd write for me,
as up where the wind was leaf-smacked
she scaled, way up and out the top of her poem.

From a Bench on Main Street in Ulysses Grant's Hometown, Galena

No freight of war reached Illinois.
Still the stardust of old artillery
collects itself on some higher plane, allowing
grief fading with history
to be confined to shadows,
dark islands beneath the maples
which in full leaf flow
toward the General's house
and sprightly tours.

Later, free of the throng
we walk from one souvenir shop to another.
Everyone reads the street for something,
except for the two lady palm readers
at card tables, who've shaken off the mystique
of scarves and drawn cheeks,
to chat and laugh about
what happened that morning
at their daughters' soccer practice.

And, so I catch myself gazing
into my own palm, searching for my country
when I look up and see a small bird flying
into the purse of a pretty tourist from Asia,
who gives a short cry,
then with tender fingertips
touches it back to the sky.

The Plump White Rat that Paul and Margie Left Behind for Back Rent

In the middle of the night
it taught me about tenants
slipping out. I did not affix
their faces to the rat,
though subconsciously I must have tried
after the rat bubbled up
like veneer over a cupboard drawer,
freezing its pose,

and Paul and Margie's blushing
features floated over it.
Or, perhaps, due to its human
connection, thought of itself
as rat above all others.
Whichever the case,
before my wife could uncrook
her elbow to hurl a shoe,

the rat had scrambled over
the drawer and cajoled
its lumpy form down where pipes
trombone beneath a sink,
and our hearts sank to meet it
in the wet rain forest
where a pipe had sprung a leak.

Later, the rat ran its tail along the baseboard,
to stress, we thought, its domestication,
and still our dreams painted it
into a corner, but how then
to catch it? A steel-jaw trap
seemed cruel for one
who'd furred in us fuzzy feelings,
even if we'd not claim them.

We settled for a cheesy cone trap
that, once inside, the rat
would become entangled,
but checking it later,
we learned the rat had wrestled
out of it, the device now
a fat fur slipper with enough fur
on the floor to make a pair.

Then from around the bathroom
it showed itself stripped down
to its skin, up on two legs,
leaning front arms against
the woodwork in a shiny bid to be human,
the plump white rat seeking
a soft eye, not taking things
personally, just trying to fit in.

Down in the Lowlands below Motel 8

Clinton, Iowa, at the train yard
the Soo Line is barely awake,
tracks laced with long sleeping giants
bedded down gray and straight,
close together
for all the freedom we imagined
them having through the countryside
and along the river.
Even the one slowly streaming
is languid, not drawing attention
to itself, considerate of late sleepers
at their sides and above them
in the motel, knowing
their glory days are absent
from the hearts of the young,
their whistles uninviting
as catcalls to the girls
and nothing to the boys
hunched over the grandeur
of video games. The trains must know
their place in this town, not mess
with more than commerce.
They must be silent
as if dead, their gray meeting
seamlessly with the sky.
In this new century
they must blend in, so the rappers
and rowdy-skinned girls
can be loud. Even the trucks
move cautiously in their midst,

as if at a wake, knowing
this is no place of wonder, one truck
in the slight dust of a whisper
as it is leaving, assuring another,
Let’s slip out of here. We’ve stayed
long enough. It will be okay
if we leave now. No one will notice;
no one will talk.

Power Lines

are always trying to pull the world tight,
bale us with wire,
place us into a spastic nerve barn.

The power lines keep good company, hanging
about with trees, connecting
to cathedrals and their vision,
inviting to birds and their twitter.
Four lines high, they disguise
a musical staff,
only to break the view at the window.

On a barren day
they tell us that we are happy
and we believe them.
Though these body snatchers
override the heart—
weighed down by a barrage of papers,
each a stone tablet,
the power lines make a playground
of the office. Telephones
hang from our ears, pencils lose
their hulls to make a point.
They rise through the hum of the computer,
lending a false sense of brightness,
which heightens the bluster
in our fingertips,
so that at night our loving is electric.
We feed out data in our embrace
like what spare part our body wants,

until at the hospital
our hearts are hooked to suction plates
and a monitor, which takes
the last of us so there's no beat at all,
not even one last song in the heart,
nothing to glean
as the lines humor themselves,
reflect upon the heart,
under the guise of refinement
move flatly, sedately across the screen.

The Old Man Under the Sidewalk

burrowed for air
on Saturday night, came up
through the tavern.
On a curbside bench he bent
over his cane, his face pinched,
tapered to a cigar,
skewing his eye stained with smoke,
who tripped me as I trailed
mother to the popcorn stand,
his eye searching from
the tip of the cane
while he wheezed, keeping me
from that kinder eye
opened and closed by the
popper lid, which promised dreams,
that everything would puff
and float, the old man ready
to cane my head, yank me
under the cement
to his dark room of loam
and worms, where his face
would nestle close,
his yellow eye breathe into mine.

The Man Who Delivered Flowers Along Leonard Street

Dangerous, it was, to be so near to love
without it touching him, to be a mere
conduit between hearts.

Few could have survived their own hands
being buried in bouquets every day
unless he had his own love at home.

All over the West Side, you'd see him—
a big moon-head of a man in his 40s—
his wide hallmark hellos

faring as well as any cheer,
then smart in his little dance of backtalk
with employees at Mickey D's.

With tulips or roses lipping forward,
stemmed to a place of honor
under his chin, he'd trot a beeline

across the intersection to some gal
in the beauty shop, a pretty head
under one of those big

lampshade-size dryers—
where she'd lip-read his leafy
whispers while her heart thumped

a woozy loop that managed somehow
to miss him altogether. Only the petals
she pressed to her bosom

could lower her chin, caught as she was
in the afterglow, with the deliverer,
in his role, floating back

from the bouquet in the harmony of
avoidance, to leave her there,
steam teaming up from her blouse,

her turned-up nose waving high
for the scent, lifting the entire side street
up from the margins.

Showdown on Carroll Street

Getting out at the Amoco to pump, connecting
the lifeline—my son still in the backseat—
I didn't sense it: behind us
on the street side of the corner house
the dangerous crowd chanting
"Shoot, shoot, shoot," men standing, tots
straddling their shoulders;
older kids lit up over cans of pop;
women, slung out in halter tops, their laughter
loud as their bare, careless midriffs.
"Shoot, shoot," once in a while the chant
collapsing on itself. A hotdog there and here,
then gunshots: a quick popping of corn.
A man inside the house, you'd learn later,
so keyed into his truck that he
wouldn't surrender it. Upstairs, holed up
at the neighbors, sharp shooters riding
the windows, maybe revolving the long
barrels of their rifles, the quietest
of propeller blades, into place,
then for effect, strafing
the aluminum siding of the house.
You imagine them with thin,
measured mustaches, each deftly working
a tree limb, culling a view. Below,
a man whose voice rises above
the others: "Come on, guy, shoot your way
out." I put back the pump nozzle,
my wallet a quick beating of wings
to help my car fly out of there.

The World's Run Wires Across the Sky for So Long Now

shedding those heavy lines would be like
shaving off eyebrows, leaving the feel

of faceless thoroughfares, despite beefs that—
along with their poles poked up

from the ground—they do not fit in,
that new lines should be buried

underground—yet waves of wires
have earned their place among leafy clutches

of trees which line the streets and pull
the eye of the driver along. Be it rush hour

or not, should folks wish to tarry, they can read
the bottoms of utility posts for yard sales

and flyers of missing pets. Most of all, I love
how transformers in a way colossal

yield to one or two wires in the country,
where poles show modesty—that they're

fine with just flicking by, letting wires
go slack like the gut of a man who knows

there's more to life than admiring a flat line
on a monitor we call a mirror. Then we,

too, relax, listen to each other, our lines
touching before we will know better.

And if a car breaks down between towns,
a yard light, the power pole's barely

recognized kin, will assist, pull the wary driver
into range, make luminous the narrow lane

between cornfields and their first frisky licks
of the night that's creeping in. If the hood

is flagged up in the grainy dusk,
a farmer with a smile curving wide like

the silver basket of silage on his shoulder
will set the basket down, call off the dogs, invite

him up under the yard light—that unassuming
post—for a good look into his eyes—

before inviting him in to meet the wife and kids
around the warm round hearth of a farm table.

Beneath Our Hickory the Blind Stranger Raps His Cane Against the Porch Screen

He has walked too long
to make it home. Dark glasses askance
(bows warped to get a handle
on his wide face),
he breathes hard his pleas
to use our bathroom.
Soon he leans on me through the door,
through the maze around
the refrigerator and stove.
Across the dining- and living rooms
I lean on his thick physique, too,
in trailing this unexpected
twist through a day so sweltering
that, heaving our way
past an old end table,
our palm prints sink through
decades of polish.
We clear the bend
at my daughter's room
(her dresser has wandered
there for us to sand),
while on our shoulders
and chests, our sweat mixes
in the wrestling out of steps.
Having squeezed through
the last tight door,
I lower him onto the toilet.
He bows his head; his glasses
leave twin pools on my arm.

I turn away, shift uneasily,
later, bear hug him up,
then watch him listen
to warm tap water
addressing the sink, close my eyes
and learn the journeying slish
of soap, hear the sliding of the bar
afterward balanced
in the chafing of skin and towel.
Finally, retracing our breath
through the labyrinth, he is out the door,
under the hickory
his hand held out too high for shaking,
as if trying to read
the braille of my face.

The Fires Actually Fought That Fall by the Volunteer Fireman

who the siren would rouse from his bed
in the middle of the night, after some wide-eyed devil
lit up another deserted barn, were not the infernos,
which the fire truck, a streak sliding sideways
around a corner and out of town,
was always too late getting to—
another barn burned to the ground.

Rather the fires fought were inside his head.
His wife still in bed and with one eye open
could see the fires, too, played out on a bedroom wall.
A long time it had been since she saw
in her husband such passion as she did
in his arms and legs flailing
in his lamp-lit fever to get dressed
and to the station, her man's shadow stretching up
into the shape of flames crowding over him.

Her eye still on him, he seemed to be extinguishing
the fires, he and his shadow fighting as one,
his mirror image, joining in, making three.
Her own shadow there too, lying beside her,
that darker side, dreaming maybe it made itself up
in the wife's mirror image and slipped out of there,
to meet up with him who made the fires—
sweetly terrible as he was—the two running through
the corn rows now, carrying empty gas cans and matches.

Learning the Names of Flowers

Each day, when my wife reaches inside
the mailbox, her eyes catch on the bright morning
glories, whose vines have twirled up the post

with glad faces. Somehow they know—better
than she—her hidden will, that it's for them
she settles a foot on every porch step,

one arm bearing the bluster of the bushes
before she lingers in her strides toward the street,
all the while maintaining an eye with irises

and white gardenias, so that I'm surprised
their spell has not swept her from our cares, drifted
her away on silky white sails. If she had,

who could blame her? Or for falling sweetly
into the funnel of a daffodil, which will not trouble
to return her. For years, I've been off-balance

in such proximity—the up, up, of their flowering
whispers and her breathing down
to them, with me sometimes wandering off,

embarrassed, going for boredom, rather than
for her hand taking mine, inviting me
to places she has entered—alone—

that soften her eyes, stir her to sighs,
so even the trees, long bystanders, believe
they are her own, and invite her to go

climbing. Oh! Let me not be
an outcast but direct my love to see in me
unfurling of a flower—inflating

the finery, if she must, unleashing
affection the heart squanders, leaving us
untaxed by our patchwork of worries.

On a Blustery November Morning in Front of His Parents' Hardware Store

a man whose mouth
has been open in awe for over forty years,
a void filled by a cigar
unlit and blindly probing.

His good looks lack
all the trimmings.
I'm in my 40s, too,
and with ragged steps attempt
to slip past him,
but the wind robs me of my cap;
I dance back for it,

and when I spin around, he's before me
with his lopsided grin,
"Uhhg," he motions, stirring
the air with his unlit stogy.

I relax into his will,
as he unbuttons the top button
of my coat,
then clutches
the collar with shaky fists,
lets go with one fist
as he fumbles into his
pocket for a lighter
and pats it into my palm.

Grasping the button side
with one hand, the hole side
with the other,
he draws me close like he
will talk tough.

Instead, when I flick
his cigar tip until it lights,
there is in the space
between us
the stillness of a church,
where no harsh wind whips or spins.

In the Parking Lot after Leaving the Mall

for Paulette,
Fairmont, Minnesota

Only after bending
does it nudge to his forehead
where he is: retrieving a feather
fallen between cars. Even then
he must catch himself
for within the plume
are remnants of flight—
the sky still contracting.

Before all flying
from the feather is gone, the mall
and the vacuous shell shock
shrink off, as does his job,
the city never his, and he discovers
he's hovering over a town.
Here his heart chanced once
its own wind and sky
to wedge under his arms,
which fluttered first,
then went flying on whim
about the shoulders of a girl
who in frilly brilliance
of fingernails—
red flash of heart,
flew back at him.

As If God Will Dress Me Down to Dust

or descend me deep into a grudge of shadows,
sometimes a bitter eye glints in me,
but soon I feel eternity flow through a horse's mane,
as it spirits across a glen
under my shirt button, as if right behind
the blowing through is the veil between this life and the last.
A backlog of belief bares as fact: God knew me
before I was born—even with my eyes unfinished,
and no spark lurked in them—when He
tussled with my bones to prop up
my heart—sumptuous breath laid out in a wreath—

as he gave my cheeks a pinch of sky to fly on,
and impulsive me nodded "Yes! Yes!"
right there in the garden, since even there the head
was first to form. But in the gruel of birth and wandering
flesh I forget: sixty odd years has the weight of 600,
though, later, realizing I, maybe, signed up for this,
I grab onto faith in the free-flowing mane
of perhaps a palomino, head jutted forth—
as if out of my chest, knowing that later,
in a struggle to mount, I'll get the vaporous push
up its flanks to perch upon its sleek back
and veer toward the hidden field.

Dusk Draws More Dark
the Closer They Approach on the Sidewalk

a Bulldog and the man who will pass as its master,
who borrows from its jowl-throbbing glory

to make his own face. The Bulldog down the street
pausing now to train this trail, lifts a back leg,

then dog and man wobble closer, the Bulldog
instead of sorting scents stares in the neighborhood

of my frame moving toward it. If the Bulldog stews—
having taken some blistering whiff of me—

I'm unaware of it, for on the strength of the sidewalk
we're guided in our roles as passers-by,

as they close the distance and my open left hand
traverses the dog's shadow in the dark.

It's bone-natural that in a person's gait the arms swing—
mine in the spirit of the maples here flowing full-leaf,

so I'm barely aware when my hand, lurching
to its most forward point, feels the Bulldog's jaws,

its steel palate tendering a force on the back
of my hand, my palm a soft lap for its tongue,

my hand fully comprehended, it seems, by thc Bulldog,
and so fluidly released that I'm barely aware

of what has occurred, my gait and that of the dog
and its man barely broken, as I proceed down the street,

strangely blessed—my hand shiny and wet—
a light chain of teeth marks around my wrist.

II.

Impressions of a Roan-Colored Steer

"[Cattle] interact with one another in complex ways,
[at times] making decisions based on altruism and compassion."
—A. Hatkoff, *Inner World of Farm Animals*

Not a runt or banished by the others to a sparse
thread of pasture, nonetheless the roan-colored steer
hung back from the feed bunk, when down its middle

I slogged through wet muzzles and salivating tongues
each dawn and dusk in a kind of crouch, a teen
tipping silage from the shiny silver basket,

while the steer stood patiently waiting a turn.
Basket in arms, I'd push back at cattle who went
beyond butting for head space at the bunk

to trying to pin their long faces over the rim
of the basket, to crash the sweet silage their way,
the cattle almost drunk on the fermented aromas

and living as if the silver basket were their only sun,
while I saw Christ in the roan-colored steer,
stalwart and assured—bearing all things

beyond any bashing he'd get later on when forsaken
and hammered into oblivion, to hang upon a hook,
where humanity grows gaunt, a kind of cross

for one of God's own, already crossed at the testicles,
then double-crossed at its horny crown,
this roan-colored steer with treetop grace

hanging back on its own terms in the shadow
of the silo these fifty years, and coming in on a curve
when gargoyle events hover over us.

When Father Castrated Hogs

the balls exploded with color:
hogshed reds to the fire beyond;
lush pinks attracted to
something pink inside a sow's mind,
some delicate pause
between snuffles and grunts.

Looking back, I believe I saw
on the pen floor
all the hog-wild tempera of love-making:
oranges which once slopped the moon;
blues turned high on their burners
like those on the water tank,
the same raving yellows fed to the corn,
and sharp greens which had
prickled their snouts,
everything which went into building
the boar's little edge on every day—
something if a boy looked at too long
his sex would go blind.
Balls, which for all their frolic,
did not breathe once upon the ground.

Plane Ride with My Uncle

The plane shadows the farm buildings,
then tipping a wing, lifts away
while I grow aloof to my other self

who, smaller and smaller, walks to the barn,
his empty milk pail turning like a bell
as if ringing in a new morning.

My uncle smiles: "How does it feel
to be above it all? I smile in return, thinking
about that other me: if he will be kicked

or his foot stepped on by the Holstein,
will it matter? Later, I hardly know him at all,
who, maybe, is only alive by static

from his clothes brushing against clothes
of other kids pouring off school buses
into the bottle neck of a pair of double doors,

my problems so small now, even if he's
bowled over by the bully tackling his zitty complexion
in the hall. Then, strangely, the bully

is seated up here with my uncle and me,
with him not seeing, it seems, the brute he is
on the ground. He smiles uneasily

but thanks me for asking him along,
as the gray metal of the plane disappears
into a gray cloud, as if only in gray

can change come, the three of us emerging,
gray geese flying God knows where,
the bully and me in a slipstream

behind my uncle, our throats
in our own bottle necks happily honking,
encouraging each other along the way.

As If a House Is Not Enough to Clean, Mother Swept the Mulberry Tree

for Dean, poking that broom
as if mulberries meant madness,
trying to sweep Dean from the tree.
Dean who would not come when called,
the purple castles staining his hand.
He laughing that mother
could not catch him in her
breathy push of broom.
The mulberry, poorly sewn,
a small throne on which to perch a life.
Mulberry with its purple so fragile
it breaks up into the parts of an ant.
Mulberry low on the totem pole of berries.
Dean low on the totem pole of sons.

While Father in the Hospital Re-Imagines His Hand

the salesman sells mother a garage full
of feed. Dust puffs from the sacks.
The noses after her business
gnaw at bags. Every complaint
grows fur and a tail.
Loneliness makes its holes.
Squeaks in the house at night
move to the garage, turn into mice
grinding through the sacks.
The small bones of their marriage
scamper across them.

She throws up her arms when she sees
the mounds of feed.
The salesman speaks quietly,
says he wanted her to have
the soft fur of security, a tail
to hold onto while her husband is away.
He says he feels trapped into
taking the feed back.
He asks for a little money,
turns his sharp face back and forth
as he loads the trucks with sacks.

Bone-to-Bone This Bouncing

on a flatbed of straw,
where I'm perched on the 7th layer—
the one that loves the sky—
on a front-row bale, a spiraling
look down onto
the tongue,

Father on the tractor, his back
to me, driving too fast
for where I sit, my soul baled loosely,
legs dangling
over the front of the load, my feet light
as if heaven's laces are already in
my shoes and ready
to be tied. But God, knot them
to this earth!

If I yell to slow down, Father will brake
hard, a chasm will
open, but it opens anyway,
as the load hits a constellation
of ruts. Front bales flying
forward—me on one—
will meet steel, tongue to flatbed tongue,
the racing gravel will catch me
up, but I reach back, way
back, farther than I can
reach, one arm growing

to the length required to grab the twine
of a bale far
behind me and close
the breech, keep the ground from baring
heaven's breath,

keep David’s harp from warping
in with salutations, the wheels
from wheeling over me
an eternity of blue pastels
with silky greens skimming my heels.

Lonely for the Old Gods
(or His Herd)

the Charolais bull, one summer, leaped
toward the sun
and when he missed,
he pulled out a stretch of fence
he tried to get loose from
with a dainty step,
but the fence grew under him,
then dragged behind
like a trailer
he tossed off for good
with a twist of hips.

Soon he trotted along the ditch,
cooling his muzzle, tail lolling,
broke east, to where the bridge
washed out one spring,
and disappeared among river trees,
inauspicious in their plenty.

For nearly a week, he wandered,
sometimes flanked by wildflowers
or mashing through the shrubby muck,
relieving his grief in inhospitable waves—
his bellow, that meaty amplifier—
cobbling storms,
sifting air currents between
his horns that had butted
too many barns.

There he stood, not balking
with head nor hoof.
On his horse, Father prodded
a course through windy silence,

caught up with him in a clearing
where the bull floated
his lonesome pendulum,
which fooled around a bit
with a breeze. First, Father
allowing him dignity, merely
watched afar the bull
in the finery of leaves,
afoot among a lace of blue stones
in that sweet ache of a place,
where he dreamed of home,
causing no fuss but pawing
the earth simply for show
or maybe refining for Father
a gift of the most
sumptuous dust.

Electric Fence

A bullet—a warning shot fired
across the prairie—
stretched slowly enough
so a steer should see
and believe,
in a lapse of lowered head
meander a step
and graze the fired shot,
like her eyes
when the stakes are low,
before you fall for her,
and she tells you,
when you brush her gaze,
to stay in your place,
and that night
you hear it
in a cricket.

Leaving Neighbors

In the deep of the afternoon, Mother, distracted
by squabbles about who got the front seat,
forgot to stop at the end of the lane,
and the Studebaker, with her inside,
and three small swallows owning the silence
on both sides of a scream but not the scream, dipped
toward the river. Though flighty, our car
seemed a safe piece of the nest—the weeds
furiously braiding themselves beneath the chassis—
with the world, a mother bird securing the nest,
aided by a towering oath of protection
in each tree. Somehow we knew
the destined elm would leap out,
the left side of the car try to climb it,
only to get caught by the rear left tire, hang there,
raised on one side, like a circus car
circling on only its right wheels in the center ring.

For Brother Bill, Collector of Old Radios

My brother passed on at 62, aficionado
of tube radios, a basement full
of old Philips and Silvertone models,
and the Crosley Companion, with high
overriding arch that suggests how wearing
nothing deeper than a doorway
of heaven would itself be transforming.

No arch, though, on the radio
in the farm kitchen growing up.
The leaky chassis with lax back panel
allowed for a city's seeping lights—
lustrous tubes, coils and filaments—
that microcosm of a place where
no clock is our keeper. There are
cool shadows, where Bill
and our earthly father walk
in the company of God, where even plants
talk and new fruit grows instantly to
replace what is plucked, and sidewalks
wander off somewhere for new delights.

My 91-year-old mother promised Bill
that she'll soon walk with them.
Good brother, whom I still see on the verge
of skin, who planned to bequeath a radio
to me but passed before he could ready
its circuitry. Still, I'll get a grip
and try to tune in news of Bill, search for
his wavelength among the waves of grain
as thermal energy knocks electrons loose.

If the band can't zero him in—I'll hold
the model of that city. Maybe God
did not bend His will for Bill, but I believe
in strange connections—all the answers
to our shimmering fears, the choppy airwaves,
the static stuttering, channeling
a lilting metropolis of angels
and saints pouring down on our ears
rich balconies of song.

12, Beneath a Harvest of Stars and Driven by Murder

I searched our grove for a grave—
that bed quickly made—
of a man killed over a girl.
Blood kicked up its heels
to learn that the shooting had occurred
past the shelterbelt
at a dance held on a makeshift floor—
ragged planks put together by a fiddle.

I brushed against grief, for no one
had slung the corpse over a horse
and hauled it home—Still, fancy
staked the claim, dwelling on where he lay
as I trod the fallen branches,
dreaming that from a low cloud
making its rounds, he'd stride to meet me,
or I'd know by limbs so knotted
it would be better off
a stump—which tree he lay beneath.

Or crickets, thick with nightly clarity,
may divulge the tree, then pondering
the girl he lost his life over, I'd try
to please—do anything
but bring it my neighbor's daughter
when its spirit lit upon her white thighs
as she glided in her tree swing.

One night, wind drifted me to the seventh tree
in the sixth row. Moss for a mouth
without moving it said get the hell out.
"You're sick with picking over things,
a boy after carrion, my corpse among them."

The wind, with leafy whimsy, agreed
but laughed it off and advised me to leave;
excited in shame, I took
windy flight down a streak of trees.

Storm

The leaves on edge, clouds
with buried match heads. You've seen
it, too: lightning strikes them, flaring
one new day, then another in the night,
days too quick to be caught by any calendar.
They flicker: yellow, incandescent, die.
No dawn, no sunset, but days all the same
mirrored in sumptuous puddles.

And since your heart is the hunter,
attentive to every shadow,
to the valor of trees, to even
the raw laundry creaking on the line,
maybe you see a boy who looks like you
step away from the wires,
and a girl, her hair not teased
beyond you but truer to the comb.
Here, as maybe the grass rallies,
you feel their shivers.
And the next afternoon
after lightning has left its scar
on an oak tree by the road,
you sit together on the school bus
and remark on the storm.

In a Fever the River Rose Over the Truss Bridge West of Emmetsburg

licking the girders, its roiling tide whipping
the roadbed, the flooding so high
that in her approach to the bridge
she must cross to reach her son at the hospital,
his hernia near bursting, and she
can hardly tell the ditches from the road
in the quarter mile approach to the bridge.
She repeats words her husband had phoned
from their son's side: "The road runs straight,
so when you're driving through the waves, aim
toward the middle of the bridge,
no matter how high the water gets."
Her eyes now steely to hold her own among
abutments and struts—she tries to keep the road
between the flying wipers—not let the wipers flick
the road off, as the front tires rise against
hope glinting in the hood ornament.

"Don't let the car float—no, don't let it float,"
she tells herself, her pupils washing
nearly away from her rivery whites,
while she pledges herself again
and again to her husband's words,
a garble now, as water slips in under
and around the doors, the water soon whispering
to her calves, her hips; she might be in
over her head—the water climbing so—
but somehow she crosses over
the bridge to be with her son,
his pain thrashing, smashing him up
against the break wall of the hospital.

And soon she’s soothing him,
as after her water broke,
when she’d pushed her way
toward him, both crying,
calling for each other in the storm.

On Summer Afternoons, Even as the Shadows Cast Their Nets

I'd get away, walk through corn rows all aflutter
to a pasture in the lowlands beside the dredge ditch,
be it under the sun or after a rain, when clay
made its mischief, clamping onto my soles
as the sun recouped, my stride breaking through the vines,
whatever fight was in them. Though puberty stewed,
trying to dedicate my flesh to shame, I'd breathe big and full,
feel the rising of my ribcage, preferring when cool winds
mixed it up, whistling through the culvert, sloughing off
horseflies before they'd affix to my flesh.

Near the stream was a towering oak, which welcomed me
with its hundred years of growth into the sky,
the boughs, thick and decisive about the many directions
it sprawled in the tree's long lope upward,
giving me solace about my leaning every which way
in my leafy thoughts. I would shinny up
and sit on the bough that was most horizontal
in its ambition and didn't insist of me spiraling perfection,
a tree never frank as a fence line about anything,
but invited me to linger, uplifted as if its own leaf.

Still, since I was me, my mind always in a squirm, like
the squirrels,
I'd try too hard to read the tree's expressions in the stream,
rivulets of its leafy ardor, light streaming
between my own branches. Though not wanting to,
I'd think about how things were going with sports
or with the girls, my flesh buzzing their debut curves,
and how shamefully my seed had convulsed
to set me free. In a wind loosely sung, the tree suggesting
into the shade that it might find reasons to stew as well,
since Christ was nailed to a tree, and Judas hung from one.

But the leaves suggested in their loll as they tinkered with wind
that I should live in grace and look for good,
though, like the oak, I was divided, as St. Paul said
about his own life: the good he should do he often failed to do,
and the bad he did not wish to do is what he did.
Then in the space framed between branches, I would find refuge,
and though a bramble was maybe sleeping in my socks,
I'd consider another seed and how it might make me
brother to a tree, feel the bounce in its bough, its limbs,
instead of trying to nail something to the wind.

Something Is Going On
Far Back of the Ancient Lawn

past the regalia of roses about the arbor
with its vines tracing the braided rivulets of the sun,
past the bird bath, that vaunted podium of robins,
and the feeder where two cardinals
and now a nuthatch have trimmed enough sky
beneath their wings to come down, no, not here
but beyond the bushes father planted for windbreaks
and a run of weeds that went to seed
and made a jungle stop short
by a fence: some of it lazy and lying down
before a dirt lane wide enough for a tractor
and baler to cross from one field to another,
not to be snagged by that fence or the one inter-
twined with roots and rusted wire, where stands
a string of plum trees you'd forget about
through the school year—where dollops
dusted by rain have filled your palm, plums
grown too big for their skin, and with teeth marks
of the sun, a glisten barely punctured,
where secretions ooze for the loll of your tongue,
past all this a view of the neighbor's farmhouse,
a screen door always banging, where a dip of a girl
in a summer skirt walks suddenly out, looks over
her shoulder to be sure no one is watching and,
hanging a hard left at the corncrib, her blouse
untucked and almost flying up, comes running.

III.

The Ascension of Sandy's Drive-In

It swirled up from its lot.
Employees had buffed bins,
refrigerators to the finest hum,
shined dispensers, milk coolers.

For months mop boys vied
for visions in the waxed floors.

Fry cooks witnessed
about some Great Rejuvenator
as they hooked tubes to vats,
at breaks read cryptic bibles
about burgers
releasing souls of cattle
at the grill.

Mothers counted how
their buoyant daughters
turned celestial,
found memos in pockets:
"No hands consort
with palms when making change."

Woody, smiling too much,
chanted over register scrolls
to a higher Sandy
as girls returned after work.
When they could have been dancing,
brandishing high heels
at all the dull senses
under the skin,

they hung around Sandy’s
cleaning tentacles
of breath from the glass,
to dip and whorl,
dreamy as dairy queen.

Tail Gator

Late night, the week of Christmas,
after hours of creeping ice,
the pavement clears.
I set the cruise at 70 and drive
while my wife reads beneath a funnel
of the darkest light,

Des Moines still afar, but sparse traffic
makes 80 West our own,
not the treacherous reach it was
when two guys inside an hour
flew by waving the middle finger—
one we passed later in the ditch—
and semis crowded our lane
and threatened, in their own way, to storm.

In the back of the van, our three children
chuckle over the teasing
they'll take at my parents' home,
where their uncle Dean
will maybe hang them by their ankles
off the banister again.

So dark that the moon
must be off celebrating.
"We're all alone out here," I intone,
and for twenty minutes I drive on,
the traffic spaced out,
nothing behind us, licking up the distance.

Then I spot in the rearview mirror,
shavings of light
on the window of the lift gate,

where headlights hold so fast
to the bumper
their light is swallowed up by something
that has to be sinister,

something so scaly
it would curdle any milky innocence
that survives someone's childhood.
I flick the heater fan off
to the sound of hissing, not from our tires
but behind them, something louder—
to let us know
we were the intruders.

A tail gator! I imagine
a tail flailing, as its jaws dwarf
the lift gate's own;
its alien eye lights grin.
I press my foot to the floor
and race back toward the world of men.

Father and I Out Driving, Not Knowing It Is the Last Time

He pulls to a stop where his car wheels catch up
to wheels of rolling prairie—silence growing louder
in lulls while rolling up the windows,

unfastening seatbelts and slamming car doors
shut. Soon I'm following him, a step behind on a wordless
path, the wind wrangling free of tombstones and their

makeshift shadows. In months I'll ponder his
diary: "68 degrees this morning, rain early
afternoon, Thanksgiving, all the kids home."

Years of spare entries—and we'd reciprocate: kisses
in the coming and going, dry and never watered,
planted on his cheeks. On this day we'd have

the remains of a rain steeped in secrets
among the sanctuaries of bones. Father and I
learned long ago, words for us seldom caught up

to love stirring, for words always wore down,
the last leaves falling, rocking uneasily, trying maybe
to concede something, so that we'd step

into each other's shadows. But he goes his way and
I, mine, what all fathers and sons know it will come to.
Suddenly Father's out of sight, hills folding

over him, as if to honor the thrift of our relationship;
ahead, graveyard stones are rounded on one end, as if
into tongues, growing confidence to speak for us.

Karla Could Ply a Smile from a Storm Cloud, Get the Sunlight to Flap Its Wings

"She's attractive as those girls on Lawrence Welk,"
my mother whispered that Friday Karla drove down
from New America to meet me at my parents' home.
When she buzzed the doorbell, it couldn't match
the buzz inside the house.
For, yes, she looked like one of those pretty maids
all in a row on my parents' program.

All weekend, the galaxy spun. With Karla
I noticed sunlight on the silverware
as we ate our muffins and jam at the kitchen window,
and how enticing was the small explosion of dice
as we played Monopoly with the family, and afterward
walked over where the Dairy Queen crowd was out,
then to the alfalfa field on the edge of town where we
parted the bristles and found the sweet spots.

To complicate Sunday, under the Lindon tree,
smiling her honeysuckle cheeks,
"If you're serious about me," Karla said,
"I will not quit my teaching job at the end of
the school year and move back to Portland."
She gazed into my eyes and pursed her lips
like she wished me to attend to them,
kiss the lipstick off her wheelhouse.

But before I could, she ripped a piece of sky
as she confessed she never thought she'd fall
for someone who wasn't handsome. I recovered quickly:
she should hold out for someone
good-looking, hold to her childhood dream.
And I, too, should wait for someone
who'd find my appearance pleasing.

The electric wires were tense, they ran
down my shoulders, arms, into my wrists.
There'd been other guys, two I'd seen
walk her arm-in-arm to her dorm.
And before that her parents hadn't locked
her door, kept the knob till she turned 18.

I didn't kiss her back to her car.
No French kiss with our tongues
in the hunt for us. I couldn't wait for her
to take a page from the wind and be gone.
I looked at Karla through a yawn, a fake one
that told her to move on.

In the summer, at my mailbox, her letter shared
what she'd done for a new guy she met,
I mulled strange things, like how intimate slivers are.
In the fall when the school year came around,
I was okay with the ironclad fog.

Mother Helps Him Up to Play Pool at Senior Citizens

Even when Father can barely stand,
it is this green sky
he loves, this topsy-turvy universe emptying
into pockets, the racking up
of the cosmos, the big shakeup
that says tomorrow
maybe he can make plans.
Hovering over a tornadic sky,
he slams the cue ball into the triangle
to rearrange the sky above him
so he won't flop like a fish
between tables. In his apartment
the world will stop, the skies
grow quiet, leaving nothing outside
the window. But at dawn he hears the break

of day miles away as a cue ball jolts
the morning into action,
those cushions—the first he's had
that push back. If only the recliner
snapped him onto his feet like that.
If only in life he could put
some English on his grunts, give them
the circuitous spin that
captivates a room, instead of
"yes" and "no" and "I told you so."

The Lutheran Church in Graettinger, Iowa, Is Burning to the Ground

Soon a mailman, three joggers, a gray-haired lady
and her poodle watch
    as smoke scuffs
the view, so the firemen
seem to lean ladders
against
the very flames they try
to put out.

A pickup driving by screeches
to a halt; backs
up;
    three men jump out, squint
through the fumes
at the swaggering
hoses, each handled
by a fireman hurrying it along.

Then suddenly the cross
begins

    to bend, as if Uri Geller,
paranormalist on TV, makes it
    swoon.
Soon the cross hangs   upside
down.

But just when the on-lookers settle
into their sighs, a Girl Scout
with a Brownie camera
she almost
drops

sees it—the cross boiling,

recoiling—

and right
before the steeple
topples—as the crowd cheers—
twists ever slowly,
impossibly back
up.

At St. Luke's Nursing Home

Mother sweeps past the deliberate buoyancy
of front desk smiles to reach Father's room.
On a clipboard on his door,
grim swings backward chart his sure decline.

She, who makes a sanctuary of his needs,
will make him lean on her
to move the mountain of one foot
before the other toward the car,

parked for now in the circle drive,
the only turnaround here,
who'll later wheel him about the store.
Hanger in hand, she turns

to hear her off-key mate,
who can hardly speak, croon in perfect pitch,
as if heaven has his voice already
at the edge of the bed,

as nurses wisp by not wearing
the caps of old, white sails hinting at another shore.
Yet beyond the end of the string
he forgets to pull for the aid

to come running is Mother, his world
on a string, who today joins him singing,
"You're nobody till somebody loves you/
you're nobody till somebody cares,"

Mother doing what the TV trying
to pull him into range fails to do,
its remote control puzzled by
the blank face of his thumb, a face fumbling

like the one between his shoulders,
which, over these last years,
has widened to an owl’s, drawing in
signals from a distancing world.

Though They Didn't Know It, the Teenage Girls Who Stole My 80-Year-Old Mother's Walker

near the courtesy desk
just inside the Safeway
must have done so to lighten their steps,
these two blurry girls
the store camera caught,
with light fingers lighter still
for the girl
who literally lifted it,
likely surprised that gravity
had almost no pull,
who the store cameras saw
with her mouth open wide,
as if from hard laughter.

It would have hobbled their outlook, for sure,
to know how it lightened
my mother's heart;
she hadn't had anything this exciting occur
since squirrels gnawed through
the webbing of her lawn chairs,
and it lightened her steps as well,
for she got along without
the walker for a week
and seemed not to miss it

until my brother bought her
a new ergonomic trigger-release walker
with a mounted pink horn
she could squeeze to blow away
suspicious pairs
of long-haired girls
with grainy faces

if she didn't throw her arms
around them and hug them
to death first.

Improbable World

A squirrel holding upright
a plastic cup, teeth clamped over
the rim, begins scaling a power pole,
stopping short for sporadic
arching of its back
in a slow procession of cup,
head, hump, and tail,
careful not to spill,
as if up there the air is so thin
the squirrel must haul up
air from the ground, hurling
upward, pausing to extend its tail
in a frilly arch, so its tip settles
a moment just behind the skull
to form a festive wreathe.
In that spirit perhaps,
it climbs to within two feet of the top
when the cup plummets.

The squirrel whirls, its head ticking down,
down, down, as it watches
the cup drop in slow cup time
built on quotients of wind and plastic width
and rim circumference,
then holds its pose—disbelief's
rigor mortis. Finally, looking
like Crocket's cap, it hurtles to the ground,
retrieves the cup, three times glances
toward the pole's daunting top,
but instead of journeying
wields its tail like a lasso,

then halts as if it's roped in the notion
it's not worth carrying the cup up
again, then with saving grace, as if
squirrel light is much too bright,
thrusts its snout
into the middle of the cup
and wears it as a lampshade.

Two Sisters

A mile from each other—
the cold shoulders of farms,

their parents' inheritance
squabbled down
to a setting sun;

after that, not a word
but disdain
balanced
with goodwill for others.

After church one widow
hailing down a car
to gush over children,
the other inside
striking up a few words
for the shy man by the hat rack.

On separate farms
at night under table light
binding quickly, as if maybe,
to outdo the unwinding:
for missions, knitting sweaters,
crocheting quilts, building
the Braille mountains.

Then failing to climb them
with their own fingers,
they'd laugh, separately,
and count it as gain.

But on town night
when they'd meet on Main,
one averted her sister's eyes
to window shop shadows,
the other awkwardly call
to someone across the street,

where nobody was,
just some lonely feeling
ghosting
parallel steps.

I'd Heard About the River of Time

but never saw where it ran through
someone's life like it did Everett Clark's.
Old Everett, bagger of groceries, had time running
quickly through his hands, lanky, middle-aged man,
with a winsome puppy grin
that hardly could let go of a face
once he'd smiled at it, only his hands
looking down at the end of the conveyor,
picking through food stuff,
bagging by weight, shape, by whether canned
or in cartons, steamy warm plastic
or cold-cut cold, his hand summoning
a thing for softness, soft as his own heart,
to see if he should set it aloft
at the top of a sack—
the bread of life breathing in his sparkling eyes
and with whomever he talked,
though he didn't talk long,

for his river rolled fast, fast, ahead of the scan,
hurrying the cashier along.
Once, following his shift when Everett
needed a ride to his apartment,
I gave him one,
and he invited me down,
his stairs steep and with a washed-out look
and grimy water line,
as if he'd descended into a dark life
equal, I was sure, to several lifetimes
in one long river to his door,
and once inside—the likes I'd never known—
floor boards lay time-sanded,

with table, chairs and lampstands bleached white
and lightweight looking
as driftwood washed onto a shore,
the walls and door with that dried-out look
of having been water-logged
as if the river in a rush to leave him behind
left not a mountain to climb,
and just as I felt despair,
Everett must have seen it coming
for he laughed richly
to depths I hadn't known were there,
and he said he was blessed to have a place of his own,
a window by his bed
that looked out onto an alley,
and with that he tapped out in the glass
a code the chained dog
across the alley
chomped down on, once he'd politely
set down his bone.

Though His Tigers' Cap Is on Backwards

this young homeowner is in the present
and looking forward, if what he's up to
the Saturday after he and his wife move into
the large white house
across the street says anything.

In a blue muscle shirt, a roll of rope
over one shoulder, he runs the ladder to the roof,
steps off onto the steepness, plants his feet, pulls back
his shoulders, thrusts out his chest
and in a swirl of sunlight seems to welcome
with outstretched arms his own luminous arrival.

For a while he stands there taking it all in,
then scales more roof,
while elm leaves, having finally shed
the tree hanging over them, do a jig on the shingles
just below him in the valley.

A hunch says he too has a dance in him
but what's he to do—disguise it
in something, for soon the dance
works its way into his legs now kicking
down shingles whipped up
at the edges, then in high leg thrusts
punts from the roof fallen branches and moss.

In roundabout strides he surveys the steep reaches,
then lassos the chimney and pulls himself up,
way up, far above a crawling cement mixer
in the heave of the street, above my own
writerly life, happy to have broken out
of the picture window,

plucks a pack of cigarettes from his shirt pocket,
knocks out a smoke, candles his thin lighter,
then sits at the peak, boot heels
to the asphalt, toes pointed up.

Old License Plates

As a child maybe out with my father,
I'd see them nailed
to garage walls or piled
in a corner behind storm windows,
and once on a showy clothesline festooned
across a sun-ripened porch
next to tomatoes.

The rain would twitch down a plate,
making some into rust-battered badges
a wall wore with honor.
Others remained untouched
by a mountain range of rust.
Some plates were shimmering covenants
between the state and the car's owner.
If it were, I might gaze at the plate
and feel my own shimmer inside,
then close my eyes and run over it
a hand, as if blind and born to Braille.

Walled plates, though, nailed
in neat rows, had the hang of the heart,
and collectors of old license plates
seemed some of the happiest
folks I would meet.
Even with no loud, honking colors,
one year's plates, with our Impala between,
reminded me that they'd taken my family
all the way to Colorado.

Just looking at the hieroglyphs
on our provincial slates,
I could almost hear a metallic click of heels
the way my Iowa and my cousins' Colorado
hit it off through us children meeting
for the first time. Though the plate
was still and stationary
on the garage wall, something in it
zoomed toward states looming
in the distance, leaving a cheer
with its charge still in the air,
its metal glazed as if dusted with
the breath of a comet or star.

Old in Our Roles of Father and Son, I Drive Father to Burr Oak Lake

the water not muscled up but placid. Silence
swells and hoards our words—slow wheels
of under current. Beneath the sun's glare we gaze
out at trees circling that shiny lure. Their branches
will soon strip to fishbones curving over water.

We stand on the bluff—so much of the lake
overlaps with pastures. Years earlier,
Mother shared the story Father kept from us—
how he and his brother once leaped across
that lake—one shiny ice chunk to another.

Now, maybe, with that story coming on—a vine
with fight in it—he motions to the small hill
where his childhood house had been. It's high
summer flying by in tall grass headed back
to the old west—only to be stopped short by gravel

and a rusty sign that from the road reads Game Preserve.
We marvel again—as when I was a child—
over wheel tracks from a stagecoach, where grass never
grew back—clay so tight, despite the long
ropey honks of geese flying over, loosening

so much in their wake. I know now—I drove there
alone! Father's spirit simply played along.
I smell the sweat of horsehide and the faint trace
of a man in a derby, reins in hand, a team
of frilly horses and stagecoach that beat a path

between the trees. In one place a rut,
where the mind sinks down on one wheel, then rises
with an axel of the carriage. For a moment
I'm not thrashed by sun in a blurring of Father
being there, who's but a fever in the weeds,

twigs sifting this in—yet I know, how in the afterlife,
all time being equal, I haven't given up on him—
his left hand intact, the right lost in a corn picker—
to step out of the coach and look around for me
after the horses shudder the stagecoach to a halt,

I'll not sway hard to extremes: If I walk into
that midst among mosquitos, nature will have me
slapping at those days, and when the coach,
a glistening spider web, is heaved upon me from
a tree branch, without a thought I will wipe it away.

How Bizarre That Snow Must Melt

When a snowman is built, like a man it has death
already in him. And strange too, that handfuls

of snow compressed and on-a-roll down a hill
or up it, whirl colossal, while the snowman's pushed

to be self-realized and luminous, collecting himself
while the child, in each breath disperses particles,

and is drab by comparison. Another child shows up.
Both match the slovenly wind, scarves flying,

all the tucks out, and wouldn't you know?—
two smaller balls in descending bulk are mounted

on the prodigious one. Hands pack them in
while the topmost ball, bare of features, collects faces

from the ones who rolled, who gift the snowman
with girth and a composite visage complete with carrot,

while each child's essence, an orb, catches
the sun's glare, then magically is like a white rabbit

pulled by its silky ears from a top hat—and just like that
the essence takes over the snowman; the hat is put

to good use. Snow watchers take heart in the flutter
of flake, that loftiest of falling, not the barbaric one

at the hands of the sun, though the child who rolled
it into life kicks it about, mindless of the higher calling.

IV.

Iowa Snowstorm

And Jim and Anna Speer,
three miles from their farm
when the white bores through them.
And Jim steps out,
eases the car from the shoulder
to keep it and the ditch
from being one thought
as his brows and mustache turn to snow.

They head for the farmhouse,
Anna's hands on the wheel,
the weather whining between their words
as she turns her will
toward him who is turning.

The car drifts toward the ditch
as the white pours into her
until the car is clairvoyant,
until it hardly matters if she veers
or if the wheel floats.

Then it matters terribly
as Jim lets go of the roadside
and the ditch slides under them,
he forgetting why he walks.

He pictures a postcard of the Alps.
How wonderful to become the snow.
But hears a cry, fumbles
through a window for the woman
and hugs her, and when he
discovers it is his wife, he is disappointed.

But he loves her, and they talk
of waiting, which they later realize
they never put into words,
and both know she is poorly clothed
to survive and he too cold
to keep from turning if he does not walk.

And they figure it's a mile
to their farm and she no boots,
so he carries her and he too tired
and small to know how,
but he does despite turning.

Any moment she will fall and
they will never get up, so they talk,
knowing while they talk, they live.
The snow blows south, and the farm is south,
so they talk south and follow their words.

Wooden Ducks

My father’s chisel skims them
close to breathing, who know
the pond of piano top
and shelf, their breath outside them,
given off by trees and seaweed
in their slow emission. In no hurry
the breath plays at windows of the house,
one day sweeping through in gusts.

Sometimes we long to be like that,
come to our body
as if we were never born
and meet ourselves in perfect wooden sleep,
behind us our poor unattached wings,
those backs of chairs, which despite
their feathery spokes and spools do not
give us rise.

But knowing this we glory
how in our flying breath
we settle there within ourselves,
while a duck slips from the carver’s hand,
bobbing, nodding,
and we know now that our maker,
often hidden, is not behind a blind
but with our beveled exhalations.

Goose Pond at Dusk

The darker it will get, the more gleam
along its wrap-around walk.
Boots punched out the glass puddles,
but the pond appears ice-locked.
My wife and I guess maybe their bills
still break through, though more often
feet web the twin soccer fields.
If the geese weren't pecking for grass,
it might look apocalyptic
when suddenly they all face the same way
as several ganders flash
a flying standstill: wings riffling
like pages of a book, as mystical
lakes, rivers and mountains shake out,
so their ranks perceive and follow.

Then a lifting in the chest—
a physicality in my shoulders beyond
the swing of arms, as small
flocks of fifteen or twenty geese give
themselves to cacophonous ascents.
Wings erupt into flight—climb
the wind's hard stairs in wide swaths
that extend beyond the park—
the geese disappearing
for moments before circling back—
testing, strengthening the rigor
of wings for 1500-mile days.

A glance at my wife, and I'm sure
she feels it too, this flexing forward
in the necks of laggard geese catching up
to the V—while bound to the walk,

no lift, only blowback, we're alert
to every rib of wind as the sky magnifies,
so I know a day comes when boxed-in
yards grow smaller still,
and we'll feel the need to push out
and rise, our arms suddenly
flappable as wings.

The Banister

Oh for the grace of banisters
hazarding even the most
broken of balconies
to take lessons from swans,
spiriting you to the top
of the stairs and down,
varnished so they do not even breathe.
Yet something bends
them up and around:
the hand knows something
the feet will never learn,
which in their heavy slur of words
fall to counting every death,
then lift up from them
in each dull, plodding step.

Meanwhile the hand lilts
over genealogies, overriding
the weariness of stairs
to learn of some eternal balustrade
where the dead hold on and ride
to some fair state.
But on this earth
the hand slides on the banister
like the harp's own wavy crest,
the spindle a fine string
that you could plunk,
as the hand, that emissary
of the heart, finds peace and promise
in the banister, which glides
faithfully past the worldly chandelier,
never halting in its healing work.

In the Wake of the Storm, When Snow Had Reached the Rooftops

my brother Dean, small enough,
crawled out through the bathroom window
and carved a path to the door.
Later, while father dug for the tractor
and loader, we cut channels so high
through the white,
that from the house to the barn
and to the pig pens and beyond,
birds winged through them
as daylight reveled,
marbling the maze's walls.

The goodwill of neighbors
after such a storm
brushed not only us but the spirit
of the cattle and hogs—
the horses as well—though,
if any livestock
cleared snow,
we never saw it. Yet time and again
they leaned in, grinning,
muzzle shivering,
nodding at the latest scoop—
be it snow or the forecast—
and finagled a way into the house
by blowing on their forelegs
to keep them warm.

We welcomed them,
as best we could, obliged:
a cow pulling up a chair
for a glass of that white stuff
we would not name;

hogs slathering in the tub, grousing
for another bar of soap
to lather up their leathery snouts;
horses fussing before the mirror
at the long faces
they had become.

Finally, with apologies
and our dogs up at 'em
and chewing on their hocks
we chased them back into
their pens—and for weeks afterward
strained to commiserate—
awkward as it was,
but this got old, and often
we'd pass so close
in those cracks into each other's life
that we'd feel their every rib
as if in cars moving
over something on the road.

The Candling

At seven, the farthest I made it past
the front door of Del's Farm Supply
was a second door deep inside,
where I was peeking through a crack
to the inner sanctum, a darkened room,
to watch the candling, where he lifted
an oval to the light.

I learned from my father, Del's friend,
that if the yolk has a distinct form, it's firm.
If there's no thin red ring nor
blood spots nor streaks, it would be crated off
with others to one of the town's
three crowning groceries.

This was magic—the kind in
which whispers are born,
Del's face caught in the glow,
with me revering his steady gaze,
while Father stood, peering over
Del's shoulder.

It's as if they were gazing up at something
more vital than the riddle of one white egg,
illumined and pristine, and upended
a moment in the mind's eye
for a lifetime afterward, way past Del and father—
both long dcad.

Seven hundred miles away and six
decades later, I lift that town to the light,
seeing now it was the oval Del examined,
Father's hand, invisible, presses
against my shoulder,

as I turn the oval over and over:
only one grocery, no hardware
no clothing store, no drugstore either,
boarded windows streaking somehow
a yolk of sun, blood-red spots maybe
from Christmas lights in April,
three antique stores with my life inside,
the tavern door open and from
within, laughter, as if to keep the town alive,
but no one's buying.

September Night, 1969

for now we see through a glass darkly, but then face to face . . .
—1 Corinthians 13:11

Toward the highest branches he cried, "Oh God!—
then bolted from the turn-off
to the pasture, "My soul is so corrupt!"
Two pals, laughing at him, leaned against the car;
another sat Indian-style on the hood—
their friend suddenly vaulting a fence into alfalfa,
outdoing hurdles that made him a track star
among ancient fields, throwing kisses
at the stones and stones at the moon.
The others, beer in hand, now serious
and spooked: "Curt, cut it out!"
Soon they were pleading his goodness,
finding at last a leafy bush, then cast
as far as a string of beers can go
into the tick of a person—each attempt,
a dry heave; their buddy cropped short
with the bluntest sideburns, he
who never careened off cushions
like a pinball scoring girls.
They thought that when he'd tire, he'd dive
into a windrow, let it go. Instead
he kept sprinting. When fatigue barred him
from squatting high, he'd continue to run,
drop a thigh into barbwire, rip out
a slag of flesh, like a deer. Then hardly
leaping, he'd shred his cheek, get up,
learn again the wages of pain—

it taking finally the three boys
and a neighbor hailed down on the gravel
to hold him or hoist him, then slide him over
those wires yet again, as the boy
whispered “Thank you” or screamed
“Leave me alone!” And a bird flew
over the field to prove
a final time there was a sky.

The Brooder House Rabbits

Unless a statute requires that the neglect be malicious, it doesn't matter that someone accused of neglecting animals didn't intend to be cruel.
—Mary Randolph, J.D., Nolo.com

At first our hands lapped waves
of fur, while their ears, long on patience,
heard out our silken hearts.
From their hutches, we gave them
over to their kind in an old
brooder house, where they bred quickly
without design, 4 becoming 70,
surely 100 if they stood to be counted,
each doe lunging into her own gut
for fur to cover the bobbing
sausages twitching out noses and ears.
Some reared to full-size in a weekend,
gaunt and wild of daylight,
grinding teeth, lungs bucking dust,
the same rabbit sometimes
doubling, so it could blame us
for its plight from two places at once.

Each day my brother and I
picked up stiff corpses.
our bodies a constant moving hearse.
The air always lame, we failed
to heal them through water—medicine
stirred in. And so, we came less and
less often with coffee cans
of water and pellets. The overflow
of containers said forget them:
there was nothing we could do.

When, finally, we’d show, skeletons
thumped a back leg of warning.
We were the monsters,
and their little eye holes
dared us to sink the worms
of our fingers in.

Leaping Doe and Fawns Flash Before Us

In foliage and street, on the fringe of this city,
deer we encroach on,
then fret over their lives spent
in a startle
we share in each encounter.

We settle for
trying to count them
instead of lingering over what it all
means when they show themselves late
and early in that interlude

when traffic's not attacking Haines Street.
On the road and through open
spaces beneath
a maple's canopy—
near the driveway we share
with neighbors—we'll spot them—
far from airy reeds and water.

Yesterday, my wife grinned before shaking
her head and saying they've been feeding
on the leafy tops of her hostas.
The deer, gone in light, bristle
through the bare stems
they leave for us.

At other times, we imagine our scent tousled
within them, as if
they're too taken with us.
One day I browsed my way back
into the stand of trees, saturated
their bony bough and antler-like
branches with my scent, hoping they'd get over
us and flee,

the doe at night impossibly hiding
fawns and herself
under the one hulking maple.

September, when leaping begins
deeper in their bones, the springing forth
flightier, the next surprise, maybe
at an apartment complex
blocks from here,
they'll be going high rise—
through a picture window reflecting
leafy spires and sky.

but for now,
doe and fawns live inside the startle,
with us trying to recover so we can count
how many in the wake of quickening
headlights,
where we settle ourselves
to number the sets of their
perked ears
that tarry for seconds
before fading.

Old Barn

May wind collapse you
but no jag of sky left from storms
be lodged into your roof,
twisting it, so you wear your roof cockeyed
like some summer hat, humoring folks
driving by, sun streaming down
to make light of barn and rafter.

Sun should hit the broadside of a barn
but within it, light should be shed
by straw alone, preserving
your dark's nurturing balm,
soothing to the fluctuations
of milking and making birth,
earning the darkness of an old museum
for boards of your pens, shiny
as if petrified from cattle rubbing
for or against them,
each for your glory, Barn,
as are light bulbs lunging
the length of their wattage
for dark they cannot touch.

Your exterior, bleached in sun,
is driftwood down some river
of time. But, Barn, at your core,
when you're dead to all
but dilapidation, swear off that river
of your dark—work it like never before.

Bring back the old farm boy,
dead, too, but for his gathering of days
into your middle. Barn,

provide a way out for him. But first
stir him to life with fear and trembling,

then marshalling your lean,
your wild creaks, your ghostly flashes
of cattle and sheep, bring on
that ferocious inevitable groan.

Backboard and Hoop

Even when it arrives at the driveway,
there's this feeling that
the boy inhabits it, that he's surged
through the long stem
of a basketball pole,
blossoming out—
his back all backboard;
his heart all hoop,
its net willing to stretch for a moment
to hold each idea
which passes through.

This boy who hates
daisies and marigolds
becoming the only flower he would be.

In one afternoon with the
aid of his father
he plants his larger self in the asphalt,
grows right up to the roof
of the garage—content now
to let his backboard shrug off
all pain, never dodge
a thing in his way.

For a while he stands there trying to believe
what he sees and feels—that he is twelve-feet tall,
his whole body branching
in fiber glass and steel.

All evening he leaps, his hands
raised in glory before himself
and dribbling out his little dance.

Matthew Schmiel

In high school he quit them all:
the touchdowns tucked under his arm,
the lumbering grunts of his
teammates' praise, their slaphappy hands,
the cheerleaders' leaps and their awe.

Drafted, he couldn't leap one barrier
toward meaning. When he broke in close combat,
they sent him home, where he hid in the house,
eating its darkness, weighing finally 400 lbs.

No and no, he'd say to me and lakes
of pole fishing. When at last he went,
his handshake slack as his cast out line
his conversation carried no hook.
Not a feature remained on his face.

For years his reflection floated the water.
Then last April, he mounted a tractor
in the backyard, steered it into his
darkest thought. When his revolver
shined like the sun, he fired into his head,
reading the Bible between each blast.

Now every night his parents dream he
paddles a rowboat into their yard, pulling up
happiness oar to oar, through the wavy
grass, through all the years he sat and sat.
Through the army and every football game
played without him he comes paddling back
to the family fold, smiling, waving a hand now,
calling from the blue skies of his brain.

The Locked Room

Even as the grand old man received kin
near his recliner in the living room,
his shiny grace nearly absolved him
of the locked room, with shushing always
winning out against any rustlings
regarding the room that had grown like a tumor
since a padlock first took stock of it,
a room no one—save him—stepped a foot in,
while Great Grandma, locked
inside her skin, sat in her chair
on a soft cushion of sadness,
eyeing the key in the hollow of his left ankle,
outlined in socks he was knee-deep in
regardless of the weather.

At gatherings, the fuss with folding chairs
not finding a place for us children to perch,
we'd be politely pushed into
the bathroom adjacent the locked room,
where we'd squat inside
the claw-footed tub or outside the rim
on which we'd balance our paper plates,
once in a while one of us getting up
to rattle the lock—quieting
the buzzing inside us.

After his tractor tipped on him
for maybe living on the steep
side of a hill, and before I'd learned
that everyone has a locked room,

my great uncle opened it,
and little he could say satisfied kin,
only that a half century of shirts and ties
were piled to the ceiling
from a half century of birthdays
and holidays, shirts pinned like butterflies—
that never fit any of his lives.

There was no mention of Great Grandma's sister,
who folks half expected never died,
but was alive inside the locked room—
the sister he left Great Grandma at home for
on fishing trips up to Minnesota,
and when Great Grandma died—
it was the same day that Kennedy was killed,
his death causing her
to be overlooked yet again,
her dying just a matter of settling
deeper into one of her sighs.

Along the Crumbling Back Sidewalk

of the surviving grocery,
the same wild, bittersweet whiffs sweep up
that emanated long ago from the concrete.
Soda and cigar butts still work their slow agreement,
where delivery men in a hurry—their dollies
piled high with Coke, Hires Root Beer,
Orange Crush, and Grape Nehi—
swing in with pop, lurch their dollies up
over the threshold—the bounce of it
occasionally catching a corner on door frames
so that crates or six packs crash to the sidewalk—
with bottles breaking, or possibly
old soda revitalized by sun or rain grates
against the gravity of the years, seeps
back up from porous concrete tempered by
decades of smashed cigar butts.
There, old soldiers at ease in the disquiet—
with shoes or boot heels yet rub out stubs
in the craggy walk, countering in concrete
that gaudy sweetness that reaches back
to cap guns and G.I. Joes, bitter offerings
of war stories rarely shared, grounded
in the walk, left outside the grocer's door.

Playing Back a Tree

After engineering a record player that could withstand playing
[a cross-section of trunk, Traubeck] filtered the input . . . into a piano track.
—Mark Teo, March 5, 2014

Beneath the needle the rings shook out a track
that ranked somewhere
between neo-classical and horror,
the grooves, maybe, with the tree and wind
wrangling out the woes of the soul
in a thunderstorm.
Forty years ago, scientists envisioned
that they would learn that trees
record every sound within their leafy sphere,
that a day would come you could play back
every creak and sigh in their rich rag-tag ascent,
and the turning over of every new leaf,
with colors revealed audibly
in the fine tuning of hues.
Not only that, but each whisper of arrow
or flap of squirrel tail
or swim trunks whipping dry from a branch
while the loose ends of some ancient love
that chipped initials in bark have little choice
but to stay, parlayed through a songbird
rooted in a gourd pitched in a tree,
and the sharp cries of a hare—
who only between the jaws
of the fox discovers it has a voice.

It Would Be Fitting for a Small Town

having pushed off on the right foot
on a long-jump board with its first store
to fly forward, feet out in front
for maybe a hundred years,
but sensing the sun's slow maintenance of shadows,
the town would begin its descent.
And fitting, too, that about then the town
would learn it's rolled out on a metal tape measure,
so that after the last grocery loses
its light, and on the door of the café
for the third time in a day
hangs a "Back in a Half Hour" sign,
to which folks have grown resigned
one long sigh at a time,
and in the barbershop,
its chair sits silent, but even in summer
a strange coldness is clipping
the air outside,
and the end can be faced,
the town would complete its long jump in the dust
and the tape snap back into its circular case.

Knowing That the Town Cop Blocks Away

poked his flashlight
into the chancy shadows along Main,
boys with little promise might linger
on the school grounds after football games,
I once among them, my face rubbed up
against the dark.

When the last lights left the lot,
we took flight up the fire escape.
As if the roof arced
with yard-line demarcations,
we made our runs along the roof's
dizzy drop-offs, stirring plummets.

In the adjacent level
the science room was a look in
at a low window.
On the lab roof we ran
to prove ourselves.

If we fell, the wind
at the whoosh of making wings
might bestow our bones
with a moment's glow—
a kind of voltage that makes us ghosts
from that night on, lingering
mid-air—no longer overlooked—
but faintly lit figures drifting
across the roof.

Far from Picnic Tables I Wander a Woodsy Edge

after James Wright

Thick with mosquitos it sinks
in whatever flesh pools they can find. Scruffy
boxelders bend through each other's boughs here,
where high weeds have hidden
a long-abandoned tennis court
I spy between swaying seed heads. I slide
down to the court on a slick of smashed grass.
If near water, it might have brought to mind
a muskrat run, which my father long ago pointed out
as a place to set traps. But I'm caught
in the back and forth of questions whizzing
as they will in secluded spots
when a man recedes to his own aloneness—
the first volley innocuous as why a tennis court
in woods and why not kept up?
But with no net, questions smack low and personal:
"Life didn't turn out, did it? Did it? Did it?—
each knit in a cricket's saw,
as the court presides with judgment
in the back and forth, my life buckled
like the asphalt, as even ragweed makes a stand
and a massive milkweed towers
from the thinnest crack, milky sap sticking
to my palm when I pull it back and still trying
to win me over when I give my head
to the cottony puffing fluff.

For Photos, Father Stretched His Right Arm Behind His Back

due to his missing hand,
hid the stump, that snatch of bone
fatted over with skin grafted
from an inner thigh.

Soon after the accident, he abandoned
his prosthetic, that plier-like contrivance.
He preferred the humanity
of a mound of flesh,
which we children, growing up
with the stump, would feel planted
on our shoulders
to commend us or give solace.

One time, at home, we might have returned
a gesture, albeit with a hand,
after his niece's two-year-old twins,
who'd been charmed by his dotage,
screamed, upon noticing the stump.
Out of embarrassment,
Mother said not to mention it.

After that day, forewarned by our porch,
its black wrought-iron railing
twisted in the twins' minds
beyond bends of the blacksmith,
they would not toddle
through the doors again, though we,
his grown children, would have
walked through walls for Father.

Yet years later, in the call of the casket,
one last time that bridge
of flesh-padded bone
returned to us, lumped in
with the shadows,
and with no one looking,
we in turn held that stump, squeezed
into it something of our own.

The Suitcase

should bear another man's initials
when it is new, not later
under the authority of a garage sale
or blistered with old tape and scuffed,
a rope tight about its belly.

With the refinement of a wrestler
I have heaved against a suitcase
until it had enough,
clasped it shut with a grunt,
offsetting the quest for grace
in some distant place.

Just once, I long to open it
not to fresh shirts and socks—
those changes in the weather—
but to a change of man,
who is refined but has the heart of an alligator,
not simply bearing a suitcase
with its hide,

but a man who has scaled
each interlace of shadows
easily in tweeds and tie
while sporting a tan.

He will slip out of my suitcase
to shake my hand, say,
"You've done a good job,
but I'll be taking it from here."
And he will, as he shakes the last
of me off, checks himself in the mirror.
At the door he'll look back with a wink
that waters me down
to my clearest satisfaction,
then disappear.

About the Author

The former poet laureate of Grand Rapids, Michigan, Rodney Torreson won the *Seattle Review's* Bentley Prize, and Storyline Press named him runner-up for the national Roerich Prize for first books. Torreson lives in Grand Rapids with his wife Paulette, where he taught at Immanuel-St. James Lutheran School for thirty-six years. In 2007, he created the online youth poetry journal, *Through the Third Eye*. In 2015, the Dyer-Ives Foundation honored him "for his longstanding commitment as a poet, teacher, patron, and advocate for poetry in West Michigan."

His three full-length collections of poetry are *The Jukebox Was the Jury of Their Love* (Finishing Line Press, 2019), *A Breathable Light,* (New Issues Press,2002), and *The Ripening of Pinstripes: Called Shots on the New York Yankees* (Story Line Press, 1998). In addition, he has published two chapbooks: *The Secrets of Fieldwork* (Finishing Line Press, 2010) and *On a Moonstruck Gravel Road* (Juniper Press, 1994). Torreson also edited an anthology, *Cultivating a Sense of Place: Poetry by West Michigan Youth,* 2009.

www.ingramcontent.com/pod-product-compliance
Lightning Source LLC
LaVergne TN
LVHW010624100826
845148LV00014B/3095

* 9 7 8 1 6 3 9 8 0 3 8 1 1 *